THE FALL TO EARTH

Joel Drake Johnson

BROADWAY PLAY PUBLISHING INC
New York
www.broadwayplaypublishing.com
info@broadwayplaypublishing.com

THE FALL TO EARTH
© Copyright 2006 Joel Drake Johnson

Cover illustration: Steve Sandstrom
First printing: October 2006
I S B N: 978-0-88145-320-1
Book design: Marie Donovan
Word processing: Microsoft Word
Typographic controls: Ventura Publisher
Typeface: Palatino
Printed and bound in the U S A

CHARACTERS & SETTING

FAY SCHORSCH, *early/mid fifties*
RACHEL BROWNEY, FAY's *daughter, late twenties/early
 thirties*
TERRY REED: *a police officer, early forties*

Place: a small American city

Time: The present

THE FALL TO EARTH was first performed on
24 March 2004 at Steppenwolf Theater in Chicago,
Illinois (Artistic Director, Martha Lavey; David
Hawkanson, Excecutive Director). The cast and
creative contributors were:

FAY ....Rondi Reed
RACHEL .... Cheryl Graeff
TERRY ....Sarah Chirapar

Director ....Rick Snyder
Set design ....Jack Magaw
Lighting design ....J R Lederle
Sound design ....Joe Cerqua
Costume design .... Alison Heryer
Staged manager .... Michelle Medvin
Dramaturg ....Curt Columbus

Thanks to Edward Sobel, Sandy Shinner, Lynn Baber, Victory Gardens Theater, Jeff Storer and Manbites Dog Theater Company, and Lisa Dillman.

for Larry B Salzmann

.

in memory of my parents
Raymond and Henrietta (Burwell) Johnson

Scene One

(A room of a typical chain motel in a small American town.
One enters the room and steps into a short hallway with
two doors: one is a closet and the other leads to a bathroom.
The short hallway leads to the bedroom area where there is
a small dresser, a chair and small table, a king size bed and
a window. A T V sits on the dresser. From outside the door,
we hear voices.)

FAY: *(Off)* Well, I can't get it.

RACHEL: *(Off)* Let me try.

FAY: *(Off)* I'm still working.

RACHEL: *(Off)* Let me.

FAY: *(Off)* I'll get it.

RACHEL: *(Off)* Okay.

FAY: Whatever happened to keys? Is this really an improvement? Does this help the world become a better place?

RACHEL: *(Off)* Pull it out.

FAY: *(Off)* What?

RACHEL: *(Off)* Pull the card out. Faster!

FAY: *(Off)* Don't yell at me. If you yell at me, it'll never get done.

RACHEL: *(Off)* But you have to—now open—here, here, here, here—

FAY: Well!!!

(The door opens.)

FAY: Heavens!!

(RACHEL *and* FAY *come in.)*

FAY: Well, it smells nice. I like the wallpaper—
oh, my gosh, there's only one bed.

RACHEL: I asked for two.

FAY: Well, they only gave us one.

RACHEL: Let's go on back.

FAY: I don't mind—

RACHEL: Lets go on back and tell them we need
two beds.

FAY: One is okay with me. It's a king size.

RACHEL: I don't think I want to sleep with you.

FAY: What's wrong with me?

RACHEL: Nothing except I don't think I can sleep with
you.

FAY: Then go back and tell them we need another bed.

RACHEL: All right.

FAY: Why can't you sleep in the same bed with me?
What's wrong with me? You don't sleep nude, do you?

RACHEL: No, I do not sleep nude.

FAY: I don't sleep nude either so we're fine with a king
size. And look how big this bed is. And look how big
the room is. This is a big room. It's like a suite. Look at
the writing desk—

RACHEL: Who are we writing to?

FAY: I might write. I might sit here and write to
someone. I might sit and just pretend to write. Look at

how you can move in this room. It's so big. Did you bring pajamas?

RACHEL: Yes.

FAY: Look how much room there is when I lie down here. I can stretch my arm out and still not hit you. Come on. Try. Lie down and stretch out and see if you can bump me.

RACHEL: I don't need to lie down. Just another bed.

FAY: Come test this one. Come lie down and test the bed.

(RACHEL *lies down on bed.*)

FAY: Now stretch out.

(As RACHEL *stretches out.)*

FAY: Look how big it is. I have more room in this bed than I ever would in a single—

RACHEL: We'd probably get two doubles—

FAY: More room than a double. You can sleep here, can't you?

RACHEL: All right, we'll stay.

FAY: I think that's the best idea. We don't want to just get here and start complaining. They'll look at us funny when we walk through the lobby. I'm taking my shoes off. I'm lying here for a little bit. You can take a shower.

RACHEL: I'm going to lie here a minute.

FAY: Then we'll both lie here.

(Silence. They both lie down.)

FAY: Are you worried about Jacob?

RACHEL: I'm sure he's okay. He likes staying with his dad.

FAY: He does?

RACHEL: He has a good time.

FAY: I bet he misses his mother.

RACHEL: He'll be fine.

FAY: I'll bet he does though.

RACHEL: He'll be okay...you know you asked me that already.

FAY: Did I?

RACHEL: On the plane. You asked me if I was worried about Jacob.

FAY: Did I? And did you give the same answer?

RACHEL: Yes.

FAY: Oh...oh, yes, you're right. I did. I remember now. And I said something about wanting to see Jacob, didn't I?

RACHEL: Yes.

(Beat)

FAY: So do you talk to Robert? Did I ask that?

RACHEL: No.

FAY: So do you?

RACHEL: As little as possible.

FAY: As little as possible?

RACHEL: When he picks up Jacob.

FAY: Ahhh.

RACHEL: We talk then.

FAY: Oh...so did you bring any pictures?

RACHEL: Of what? Of Jacob?

FAY: Yes.

RACHEL: No. I'm sorry.

FAY: You didn't bring me a picture?

RACHEL: I was in a hurry—

FAY: You don't have one picture of my grandson with you?

RACHEL: No.

FAY: How can you leave town without one picture of your son?

RACHEL: I don't know—

FAY: You should have brought me a picture.

RACHEL: I'll mail one to you.

FAY: You can only spare one picture?

RACHEL: I'll mail you five pictures.

FAY: You'll forget.

RACHEL: I won't forget.

FAY: You're prone to forgetfulness.

RACHEL: I'm not.

FAY: You are.

(RACHEL *turns on side away from* FAY.)

FAY: Hmmm.

RACHEL: What?

FAY: Nothing.

RACHEL: What?

FAY: I just hmmmed. *(Beat)* I love to stay in motels. I can lie here and not worry about anything. A maid is going to make the bed and clean the room. If I get hungry, it means I have to go to a restaurant to eat. I don't have to cook and I don't have to try to please anyone. Your dad can be so hard to please when it comes to cooking. There are certain things he doesn't like. He doesn't like fish for one thing. I like fish, but I can't ever have any unless I make him something else and who wants to do that? Although I suppose I could. I could make two different meats and then serve the same vegetable. Broccoli goes with anything. But then your dad doesn't like broccoli so there goes that idea. Not that there aren't hundreds of kinds of vegetables. But when you go to a restaurant, you can order whatever's on the menu. I think tonight I'll have fish. *(Sitting up)* I wonder if they have room service here.

RACHEL: I would imagine they do. They have a twenty-four hour restaurant.

FAY: Do they? *(Getting off the bed)* There must be something here. *(At desk)* Did you see this pretty stationary? I'll have to take this with me. *(She takes the stationary and puts it in her purse.)* This will be nice to have. A souvenir. *(Beat)* It's okay to take a souvenir, isn't it?

RACHEL: It's okay.

FAY: I was just thinking that... *(Reading)* "Room Service". Ohhh, this is a nice menu. And they have a fish sandwich. And they have fried catfish. I love fried catfish. Maybe we'll have room service later and I'll order catfish. I'll bet they caught it near by so it will be fresh. Look at the desserts. I always think it's funny that restaurants have a dessert menu like everybody has desserts after their meal. That's something I've never done. Do you find that? That everybody has desserts after a meal?

RACHEL: No. Just for special events.

FAY: I suppose eating out is usually a special event. You don't think of eating out just as a way to eat, but as a special time...unless you're rich which I am not. *(She chuckles.)* I guess this is one of those special times.

RACHEL: Are you going to be all right?

FAY: Me?

RACHEL: No, the other person in the room.

FAY: The other— *(She chuckles.)* I'm okay. I'm just a fish out of water. *(She chuckles.)* I'm just a catfish out of water.

RACHEL: You don't have to go with me if you don't want to.

FAY: Oh, I'm going.

RACHEL: But you don't have to.

FAY: You're not going by yourself.

RACHEL: But I want you to have the option.

FAY: I don't need an option. I'm going and that's all. *(Beat)* Where does this door go?

RACHEL: The other room.

FAY: The other room?

RACHEL: Don't open it.

FAY: *(As she opens the door)* I'm just going to see. Oh! Another door.

RACHEL: Don't—

FAY: It's locked.

RACHEL: There might be someone in there.

FAY: Oh, do you think?

RACHEL: There might be. Close the door and lock it. Mom—

FAY: I'm just checking. Let me check the other door—it's locked.

RACHEL: You'd think you'd never been in a motel room.

FAY: I've been in motels.

RACHEL: But you'd think...never mind.

FAY: What?

RACHEL: Never mind.

FAY: You know, if your dad had come, we could have stayed in this room and you in the next.

RACHEL: If Dad had come, I wouldn't be here.

FAY: Really?

RACHEL: It wouldn't have been necessary.

FAY: You wouldn't have come?

RACHEL: I would have come, but it wouldn't have been necessary. That's all I meant.

FAY: But you said you wouldn't have come.

RACHEL: I would have come.

FAY: But you said—

RACHEL: Why don't you lie back down?

FAY: Would you have come?

RACHEL: I just said yes.

FAY: Oh...why wouldn't this have been important enough?

RACHEL: Yes...I said, yes! Did you hear me say yes?

FAY: I also heard that it wouldn't have been necessary—

RACHEL: Oh, God.

(Beat)

FAY: *(Very softly)* I heard that, too. *(Beat)* Can we really sleep right now?

RACHEL: We're relaxing.

FAY: Oh...Okay...

(She lies back down. There's a pause.)

RACHEL: I'm sorry that I—I'm sorry. I don't want to snap at you.

FAY: Then don't...tell me a story.

RACHEL: I have no stories.

FAY: No stories? You live in Chicago and you don't have one story?

RACHEL: No stories. Sorry.

FAY: Hmmm...I thought our plane ride was good.

RACHEL: Mmmm.

FAY: And business class, that was so nice. I'd never flown business class—that was nice of you to do that—

RACHEL: I didn't have to pay. I have plenty of mileage.

FAY: But it was nice of you to do it, anyway. I felt very businesslike. I was worried I'd feel out of place, you know, since I'm not really business class, but everybody seemed so nice. Not snobbish at all. *(She chuckles.)*

RACHEL: What?

FAY: I was just thinking that I may have overdressed a little.

RACHEL: You look nice.

FAY: But I thought I should dress up more since I was flying business class. I thought I should look like I meant business.

RACHEL: And you did.

FAY: Did I?

RACHEL: Yes.

FAY: This outfit is okay, I suppose. Can you tell it was from Penny's?

RACHEL: No.

FAY: Really?

RACHEL: No, I couldn't tell. It wouldn't have mattered, anyway.

FAY: I shouldn't buy from Penny's, probably. Their stuff falls apart after the first wash. But I like going there. I like Penny's. The flight attendants were very nice. A little wine during lunch. That was nice. I even got a little high. Could you tell?

RACHEL: No.

FAY: Really?

RACHEL: I couldn't tell.

FAY: Good...what was his name?

RACHEL: Who?

FAY: Our flight attendant.

RACHEL: I don't remember.

FAY: Todd, that's right. Todd. Todd is, what? Irish?

RACHEL: I think so.

FAY: Richard Todd was Irish. The actor? Richard Todd?

RACHEL: Ahh.

FAY: But that doesn't mean our Todd was Irish, I suppose...but what a nice man...did you notice the little flecks of blonde in his hair?

RACHEL: No.

FAY: There were little flecks of blonde. I think he must get it touched up...it was pretty...I thought about asking him, but was too nervous...I wanted to tell him he had pretty hair, but wasn't sure he'd like that... and the plane was...nice...so roomy...I didn't like the turbulence...scared me a little bit...I was thinking about

crashing...I thought if we start to crash, I'll die before
we hit. I'll die of fright. My heart will give out. I hope
my heart will give out. I hope it will give out quickly,
painlessly but then I thought: be careful what you wish
for. You don't want to die of a heart attack and then
have the plane land safely on the ground. I've read
stories, newspaper stories about those last minutes,
how horrible it is, spinning, out of control. Sometimes
people fly out of their seats...some people cling to the
person next to them. Whisper final words...I love you,
they say. I love you. I don't know you, but I love you.
I couldn't stand you for the last ten years, but now I
love you. I used to like you, now I love you. You're
not very pretty, but now I think you're beautiful and I
love you...suitcases, souvenirs, vomit and babies flying
through the air and they whisper, I love you...I wonder
if you can cling to one another as you get thrown
through the air. I wonder if you can hold on that tight.
Probably not...unless you're in business class...with
Todd. *(She chuckles.)* Relaxing?

RACHEL: Yes.

FAY: But not asleep?

RACHEL: No.

FAY: Do you want me to be quiet?

RACHEL: No.

FAY: Hmmm...okay... Do you believe in heaven?

RACHEL: No.

FAY: Oh... So you won't see me again after I die....
Did you hear me?

RACHEL: Yes.

FAY: You won't see me again if you don't believe in
heaven. I'll die, then you'll die and we won't see each
other again. I'll be up in heaven looking around for you

and then some angel will come up to me and say: oh, you know, your daughter won't be here. She didn't believe.

RACHEL: Who could believe in all that shit?

FAY: Well...hmph... Shit?

RACHEL: Yes...you?

FAY: I try to believe. Then I start thinking about all the people who have died—how could there be room for that many people? Unless we're reduced to the size of a molecule. But when I don't think about the practical side of things, yes, I believe in heaven. Right now, I'm thinking of the practical side of things and so I don't believe in heaven and that seems okay with me, really...sometimes as I drive to work, I think about dying and think how nice it might be because I'm feeling so tired. I don't know what that makes me. A depressive non Christian, I suppose, which is getting easier and easier for me to accept. Of course, there's no sense in being a Christian if you don't believe in heaven, because that's your great reward for taking on the struggle. As if we don't feel small enough as it is without being reduced to the size of a molecule for the rest of eternity, right? *(She chuckles.)* Your dad once said that he didn't believe in God until he met me.

RACHEL: That's sweet.

FAY: That is sweet.... I don't think your dad could take it.

RACHEL: No.

FAY: I don't think he could. Your dad likes to sit on the couch now. And watch the news. And he especially likes watching the dregs, you know, the murders, the rapists. He likes that. The other stuff, the stuff on Afghan or Africa or Asia or AIDS doesn't interest him, but he loves the dregs. The explosions going off everywhere. He's got that little tummy now. Tummies, that's what's wrong with my generation. All the little tummies we've got hanging there. I tell your dad, "Ed, you're beautiful; it's just your tummy." That's your dad. He said to say hello.

RACHEL: He didn't say that.

FAY: He did.

RACHEL: Right.

FAY: He said say hello to Rachel and tell her I love her.

RACHEL: Right.

FAY: He's not so bad.... He's not.... Rachel, he's not so bad. He said to me, you know what he said to me?

RACHEL: What?

FAY: He said: fathers miss their daughters. Their sons, they don't miss. But they always miss their daughters.... So we go down...

RACHEL: What?

FAY: So we go down to the police station...

RACHEL: I think it's the morgue—

FAY: The morgue...we go to the morgue...so we'll see him?

RACHEL: Yes.

FAY: We'll see him...hmmph, Kenny...it's been three years since I've seen him...were you there?

RACHEL: What?

FAY: The last time he was home? Were you there?

RACHEL: No.

FAY: So it's been even longer for you.

RACHEL: Yes.

FAY: Hmph... Your dad kept crying and crying... he couldn't take it.

RACHEL: He should have come with you.

FAY: He couldn't take it.

RACHEL: And you can?

FAY: I can take it. Your dad can't take things—I don't know why. He fought in Viet Nam. You would think he could take it. What could be worse?

RACHEL: *(Softly)* I don't know.

FAY: What?

RACHEL: I said I don't know.

FAY: Me, either...do you remember when the bat got in the house and it flew all over the living room?

RACHEL: Yes.

FAY: And here I am chasing the bat with a broom and your dad runs to the bathroom and shuts the door. I chased that bat until I killed him. Until I beat the thing silly...it was fun, really.

RACHEL: It was fun?

FAY: I sort of enjoyed it once I got over my fright. It scared me at first because I didn't know what it was, it was just a black thing flying through the air and it scared me, but once I knew it was a harmless bat and I had picked up my broom to kill it, I wasn't scared at all. I just went after it. And he went after me, too, once he figured out what I was up to. You and your brother were off in a corner screaming and—I suppose that's what did it. That's what made me lose my fright. You and your brother off in the corner, screaming. And you were screaming: don't let it get in my hair! You had long hair then—

(RACHEL *chuckles*.)

FAY: And when your dad shut himself in the bathroom, you and your brother laughed. And I chased that poor bat around and around and we all laughed and screamed...until I finally beat it to the floor—he came after me at one point, but I beat it and beat it. And your poor dad—

RACHEL: Poor dad.

FAY: Scared to death.

RACHEL: He still should have come with you.

FAY: He couldn't take it.

RACHEL: He still should have come.

FAY: Don't pick on your dad.

RACHEL: I'm not picking on him.

FAY: You are. You always have—

RACHEL: I didn't—

FAY: You did.

RACHEL: He should have come with you!

FAY: *(Angrily, loudly)* Well, so he didn't, did he?

(Beat. FAY gets off the bed.)

FAY: *(Softly)* And then I picked it up and I buried it out in the backyard. The bat out of hell. *(Beat. Going to window)* Lets see if we have a view. *(She opens the curtains.)* We do. There's trees and mountains beyond the parking lot. I wouldn't mind driving out there. I've never been in the mountains and I wouldn't mind seeing a little of it before we leave. Could we do that?

RACHEL: Sure.

FAY: How much mileage do we get on the car?

RACHEL: Unlimited.

FAY: Unlimited? Unlimited? That's what I like. I like unlimited. Well, then we should go further than those mountains. We should go to the other side. Unlimited?

RACHEL: We got a special deal.

FAY: Then we should drive all over the place. I could use a little natural beauty right now.... Do you get lonely, Rachel?

RACHEL: I...I suppose I do.

FAY: Since the divorce.

RACHEL: Some.

FAY: Me, too. Your dad sometimes just sits there reading a really bad book while his tummy grows and grows. I just want to slap him sometimes. Put him in a nursing home. You stay here, I want to say, while I get on with my life. *(Looking out window)* We must be the only people here. No other cars. No, I don't see one other car.

RACHEL: *(Getting off the bed)* I'm going to unpack.

FAY: Oh...I suppose I should, too.

RACHEL: You don't have to.

FAY: But I want to.

(They both begin to unpack...)

RACHEL: Which drawer do you want?

FAY: I don't care.

RACHEL: Take the top one.

FAY: I'll take the top one, then.

(They unpack.)

FAY: I'll hang this up. Maybe we should wipe out those drawers.

RACHEL: I think they're fine.

FAY: You think they are?

RACHEL: I think they're fine.

FAY: You have anything to hang up?

RACHEL: I can do it.

FAY: Okay. What is that?

RACHEL: A bra.

FAY: A bra?

RACHEL: Yes.

FAY: They make bras like that?

RACHEL: Yes.

FAY: Let me see that.

RACHEL: No.

FAY: Let me see that thing.

(RACHEL hands it to her.)

FAY: Why, it's hardly anything.

RACHEL: That's the point.

FAY: I couldn't wear it.

RACHEL: Yes, you could.

(FAY sniffs it.)

RACHEL: Don't smell my bra! What are you doing?

FAY: Just checking it out.

RACHEL: Did you have to smell it? Jesus.

FAY: I wonder if I could wear something like this.

RACHEL: I'll take you shopping.

FAY: What else do you have there?

RACHEL: Nothing. You are not going through all my clothes.

FAY: I thought if you have anything interesting.

RACHEL: I don't.

FAY: Oh, there's that little phone.

RACHEL: Cell phone.

FAY: You brought your cell phone? Look at that little thing. Let me see it.

(RACHEL *hands it to her.*)

FAY: I've never seen one this small.

RACHEL: Most of them are that small. Don't smell it, okay?

FAY: *(Laughing)* I won't smell your cell phone. *(As she pushes a button or two)* What is all this—

(RACHEL *takes it from her.*)

FAY: Did I break a secret code?

RACHEL: No.

FAY: The way you grabbed it, I thought I'd broken a secret code.

RACHEL: It's important to me, that's all.

FAY: Oh. An important cell phone.

RACHEL: Yes.

FAY: Why did you bring your cell phone?

RACHEL: So I could call Jacob tonight.

FAY: But there's a phone in here.

RACHEL: It's cheaper and faster—

FAY: Is it? It's cheaper—

RACHEL: And faster.

FAY: But are there codes? Do you have codes?

RACHEL: No, Mom, no codes.

FAY: You big liar.

RACHEL: Okay, there's a secret code and I'm not giving it to you.

FAY: Big liar. So do you use it a lot?

RACHEL: Yes. I take it everywhere I go.

FAY: Really.

RACHEL: Yes.

FAY: So you could call me anytime.

RACHEL: I—

FAY: You carry a phone with you, all the time, and yet I certainly never hear from you, even though you could call me anytime.

RACHEL: It's mostly for business—

FAY: Ahhh, business. Business. Well, it's certainly fancy—too fancy for these hands, I guess. My ears. I bet Jacob loves it when you call him on this phone.

RACHEL: As a matter of fact, he does.

(Beat)

FAY: *(Going into* RACHEL's *suitcase again.)* I bet this blouse wasn't cheaper and faster.

RACHEL: Would you stop it? Stop it.

FAY: All right.

(As RACHEL *begins to go through* FAY's *suitcase.)*

FAY: What are you—you get out of there—

RACHEL: *(As she goes through* FAY's *suitcase.)* Now show me *your* bra.

FAY: What!!??

RACHEL: You're so nosy. I'm nosy, too. Show me your bra.

FAY: You're not interested in my bra.

RACHEL: I am. I want to see your bra. Let me smell your bra.

FAY: *(Giggling)* I'm not letting you smell my old bras—

RACHEL *(Bringing out a bra)* Well, would you look at this—

FAY: Stop it now. Rachel. Stop it. You silly thing....you can be so silly... *(She giggles.)* ...My old bras....Whoops!!! Whoops! Forgot my toothpaste. Forgot my toothpaste and my toothbrush. Oh, for heaven sake.

RACHEL: We can buy it here.

FAY: We can?

RACHEL: They have stores here, too.

FAY: That's true. I want to brush my teeth.

RACHEL: There's a gift shop.

FAY: Is there a gift shop?

RACHEL: In the lobby.

FAY: I didn't see one.

RACHEL: It's in the lobby.

FAY: I should go down—

RACHEL: Right now?

FAY: I want to brush my teeth.

RACHEL: I'll go down.

FAY: You don't have to. I can wait.

RACHEL: I'll go now.

FAY: My teeth feel grungy.

RACHEL: I'll go right now.

FAY: I'll go with you.

RACHEL: You finish unpacking.

FAY: I like a whitener.

RACHEL: A whitener?

FAY: If they have it. And soft bristles. My dentist said to only brush with soft bristles because my gums are sensitive. You, too. He said everyone should brush with soft bristles.

RACHEL: I'll be back in a second.

FAY: Well, I could—

RACHEL: I'll be back in a minute. *(She leaves.)*

FAY: *(As* RACHEL *closes the door)* Well, if you want... hmph...oh! *(She runs to door as—)* I've got money, here. *(She opens the door.)* Rachel? Hmmm...give it to her when she comes back. *(She looks over the room.)* Well... *(She begins to put things away.)* Probably wanted to get away from me for a minute—you don't know that— oh, yes, I do! She never comes home, does she? ...Don't let yourself get down, Fay. Don't let yourself get down. Don't let yourself. Don't let yourself... *(As she pinches herself)* Pinch. Pinch. Pinch—oh no, that's for giggling. *(She goes to mirror and looks at herself.)* Okay, now listen, Fay, this is what you do. This is what you do. You think of what must be done, be done to get through. That is what you do. You look strong now. You look strong. *(She is obviously fighting not to cry.)* Would it help to call Ed? Would that help? I don't know. I don't know. I don't think that's a good idea. He'll cry. He'll just cry...But I like this room!! I like the big bed! I like the secret door! And I like this view! You lived in pretty country, Kenny. Very pretty country. *(She begins to hum* Dancing in the Streets *a bit in a semi-agitated way. She hears something near the door to adjoining room. She freezes. Beat. She tries the inner door, but it's locked. She puts her ear to the door. Nothing. She sits on bed trying her best not to cry.)* Get it out now! Get it out now! Get it out! *(She gets up suddenly.)* It wouldn't have been necessary, she says! It wouldn't have been necessary! *(She goes to* RACHEL's *suitcase and finds the cell phone.)* You'd come if it was necessary! *(The phone rings.)* Well! *(As she tries to answer it.)* Hello? Well, for heaven sake. I don't have the code! I don't have the secret code!!! Hello? Oh. Well, no, she's...I'm the mother. I'm her mother. Well, yes, I will. And how do you spell that? T-H-O-M-A-S. And your last name? How do you spell that? C-O-N-W-A-Y. Yes, I will tell her. Is this a business call? Personal? Oh. Thank you. Good bye. *(Beat. She stares at the phone. Then she goes to the window, opens it after a struggle and throws the cell out the window.)* Fucking cell phone. There goes the fucking cell phone! *(Beat)* Oh, my God! Oh, my God, what have I done? You're crazy, Fay, you're crazy. She'll kill you is what she'll do. I should go down and get it. You should go down and get that thing. Oh God. Oh, God.

(She lies back on the bed. She begins to sing "Dancing in the Streets" as RACHEL *comes in.* FAY *doesn't see or hear her and continues singing. With a small sack in hand,* RACHEL *stands at the door and listens. She does not move until* FAY *finishes singing. Then quickly opens and closes the door.)*

RACHEL: *(Standing at door and still out of* FAY's *sight)* Toothpaste with whitener!! And a soft bristle toothbrush!!!

(Beat)

FAY: *(As she sits up)* Then I guess I'll brush my teeth!

(The lights blackout.)

Scene Two

(An office of police station. FAY, RACHEL, *and* TERRY, *a police investigator.* TERRY *sits behind a desk.* FAY *and* RACHEL *sit in chairs in front of the desk.)*

TERRY: I can't imagine what a difficult time this must be.

FAY: It is difficult.

TERRY: I'm sure.

FAY: It's hard to imagine unless it has happened to you as well.

TERRY: Yes.

FAY: Losing a child. Have you lost a child?

TERRY: No, thank God.

FAY: Yes, thank God. They say that terrible things happen to families that lose a child. Have you heard that?

TERRY: I have, yes.

FAY: Terrible things.

(Beat)

TERRY: Can I get you anything?

FAY: What do you have?

TERRY: Oh...ahh...coffee—

FAY: I'd like a cup of coffee.

TERRY: Water.

FAY: I'd like a glass of water, too.

TERRY: And some soft drinks.

FAY: What kind?

TERRY: I'd have to go out and look.

FAY: Just water and coffee for me.

RACHEL: Nothing, thank you.

TERRY: Do you want anything in your coffee?

FAY: What? Oh, no. No, just the water and the coffee.
A little ice in the coffee?

TERRY: Ice?

FAY: To cool it off. I worry about hot coffee spilling.

TERRY: I don't think we have any ice.

RACHEL: She doesn't need any ice—

FAY: *(Cutting in)* I don't need any ice.

TERRY: *(As she exits)* I'll be right back.

FAY: You live in very pretty country.

TERRY: *(Stopping)* Oh...I think so, too.

(She exits. Silence)

FAY: Hmph...hmph...hmph...

RACHEL: What?

FAY: Nothing.

RACHEL: You're okay?

FAY: Yes...let me decide if I need ice or not. Okay?
Let me decide.

RACHEL: All right. I'm sorry.

FAY: It shouldn't irritate you so much if I—

RACHEL: It didn't—

FAY: It irritated you. *(Beat)* What does it cost to send a
body home?

RACHEL: I don't know. Not that much, I wouldn't think.

FAY: No?

RACHEL: I'll pay for it.

FAY: We can pay for it.

RACHEL: I'll pay for it.

FAY: We can. I got a raise at work. Stanley told me the office would fall apart if I wasn't there—

RACHEL: That's nice—

FAY: So he gave me a raise.

RACHEL: But I'm paying for it.

FAY: Why is that?

RACHEL: I just want to.

FAY: All right...thank you. *(She leans into desk to peak at the papers* TERRY *has left there. Beat)* What does that say there?

RACHEL: Lets wait for the officer.

FAY: It says suicide, I think. Suicide? What is that? Suicide? *(She has gotten up and picked up report.)* Did you know it was suicide?

*(*TERRY *comes in with coffee and water.)*

FAY: I notice it says suicide.

RACHEL: Come back and sit, Mom.

TERRY: *(Overlapping with the above)* Let me put this down.

FAY: I don't get it. *(To* RACHEL*)* Did you know?

RACHEL: Yes.

FAY: But you didn't say—

TERRY: May I have the report back, Mrs Schorsch?

RACHEL: *(Overlapping)* I thought it should wait.
Give back the report.

FAY: You thought it should wait?

RACHEL: Yes. Give back the report.

FAY: Why? Why should it wait?

RACHEL: I don't know—

TERRY: Your daughter probably thought it would
be best—

FAY: Best for what? I don't get it. I don't get it.
(To RACHEL*)* You said you didn't know. Exact words.
You didn't know. Ohhh, God, I have to say this to Ed.
I have to tell Ed his son killed himself. I can't do it.

RACHEL: I couldn't either.

FAY: But I can take it. Your dad can't take things.
I can take things.

TERRY: I'm so sorry, Mrs Schorsch.

FAY: I know you are. I know. You look like a sweet
person. You look sweet—

RACHEL: Mom—

FAY: Oh, Kenny, Kenny, Kenny. Kenny, Kenny, Kenny.
You should have told me—

RACHEL: I'm sorry—

FAY: *(As she gives back the report)* I don't like doing
this in here. I don't know this person—you seem like
a sweet person—but I don't know you.

TERRY: Should I leave you alone?

FAY: If I had been home, I could have hid in the
bathroom until I composed myself. *(To* RACHEL*)* When
you called the first time, I hid myself in the bathroom
until I was composed, enough to tell your dad. I should

be in the bathroom right now, Rachel. Until I'm
composed and I'm ready.

TERRY: *(Getting up)* I'll leave the two of you.

FAY: No, no, I want to hear. I want to hear. I won't
drink my coffee. That would be crazy. To drink coffee
would be absolutely crazy, but I would like to hear now.

FAY: *(To* RACHEL*)* I know you didn't mean anything,
did you?

RACHEL: No.

FAY: You didn't mean for this to happen, did you?

RACHEL: No.

FAY: I know you didn't. I thought he'd just died.
I thought maybe it was a heart attack, I don't know.
Why I thought that, I don't know. He was barely thirty.
People don't have heart attacks when they are barely
thirty, but he drank and I knew that. I knew he drank.
I thought maybe he had been killed in a car accident.
Remember, Rachel? I asked that.

RACHEL: Yes.

FAY: And you said you didn't know.

RACHEL: *(Overlapping with above)* And I said I didn't
know.

FAY & RACHEL: That they wouldn't tell you [me].

FAY: So you lied, but I understand why. I understand.

TERRY: What can I do for you, Mrs Schorsch?

FAY: Oh gosh, nothing, I suppose. Nothing. Go ahead.
I'm not sure what should happen next.

TERRY: Well—

FAY: Where is he now?

TERRY: Downstairs. We can go down—

RACHEL: I'll go down. You can stay here.

FAY: Not in your life. I'm going down. I don't care.
I'm going to see Kenny. I'm going to see him. It's been
three year, you know. I'm going to see him. *(To* TERRY)
Do you have kids?

TERRY: Yes.

FAY: I thought so. You look like a mother. How many?

TERRY: I have two.

FAY: So you understand?

TERRY: Yes.

FAY: I should go down. I should see him. It's a mother's
duty, a mother's right to identify her children.

TERRY: I understand.

FAY: How old are your kids?

TERRY: Ummm...oh, gosh, I've forgotten, they're,
ummm, seven and ten. Seven year old boy and a
ten year old girl.

FAY: It's nice when the girl is older. Rachel is older.
One year. So I know how nice it is to have a daughter
who is older. I'm not sure Rachel liked being the
oldest—did you like being the oldest?

RACHEL: It was fine.

FAY: She obviously did not like it.

RACHEL: I said it was fine.

FAY: She was always very helpful. Your daughter, too?

TERRY: Yes.

FAY: She helps take care of her brother.

TERRY: Yes.

FAY: That's good. It makes a difference.

TERRY: *(Hesitantly)* My son has a reading problem.

FAY: Oh.

TERRY: And she's very good in school. She helps him out with his school work.

FAY: Homework! Just one more reason to have an older daughter. *(Matter of factly)* So how did it happen?

TERRY: What?

FAY: He killed himself how?

TERRY: A rifle.

FAY: A rifle. How exactly?

TERRY: Through the mouth.

FAY: Through the mouth?

TERRY: He put the rifle in his mouth—

FAY: So he meant to do it. He meant to make no mistake.

TERRY: Yes.

FAY: Hmph.

TERRY: He rented a motel room.

FAY: Oh. He went to a motel?

TERRY: He checked in at 12:01 in the morning. At approximately 12:15 A M, the people in the adjoining room heard a gun go off and called the night clerk who called us. We arrived about eight minutes later, knocked at the door and then had the night clerk let us in.

FAY: Yes.

TERRY: Your son was found on the bed—

FAY: You were there?

TERRY: Yes.

FAY: What did you see? I want to know what you saw.

RACHEL: We don't need to know what she saw.

FAY: I need to know.

TERRY: Some people want to know and some people don't. Most people don't.

FAY: I want to know. *(To* RACHEL*)* You don't have to stay.

RACHEL: I'll stay.

FAY: You can stand in the hallway.

RACHEL: I can take things, Mom.

FAY: That's right. I forgot. *(To* TERRY*)* What did you see?

TERRY: He had been sitting on the edge of the bed. He had placed the gun butt on the floor and wedge it between a magazine stand and some books. And then leaned into it putting the rifle into his mouth and pulling the trigger. The impact had thrown him back some—

FAY: He died quickly.

TERRY: Very quickly.

FAY: There was a lot of blood?

TERRY: There was quite a bit.

FAY: On the walls, I suppose.

TERRY: There was some. Mostly...

FAY: Yes?

TERRY: *(Quietly)* Mostly soaked in the sheets. The mattress got most of it.

FAY: Oh.

TERRY: It was pretty soaked through. I was with Frank, Frank Melcher and he—

FAY: Frank is who?

TERRY: A policeman. He got the first call. He's a good man, Frank. A sweet man. A sweet man for a cop and he was real careful with lifting your son. No rough stuff with Frank. He's not like that.

FAY: Melcher. That's what? Swedish? German?

RACHEL: It sounds Swedish.

FAY: Does it?

RACHEL:	TERRY: *(Simultaneously)*
He looks a little Swedish.	It could be German.

FAY: Oh.

TERRY: We had to check, I had to check to make sure, as an investigation, that it was a suicide. I had to make absolutely sure. And it was. It was absolute.

FAY: Oh.

TERRY: There was two fragments from the skull. That were found.

FAY: Ahh.

TERRY: I don't know how much you want to hear—

FAY: Was the T V on?

TERRY: Yes.

FAY: I thought so. I thought it must be. Kenny liked to have the T V on. All the time. But he died very quickly?

TERRY: Yes.

FAY: Instantly?

TERRY: Yes.

FAY: What was playing on the T V?

TERRY: Oh...I don't know...I can't remember.

FAY: Probably a nature show. He loved shows about nature. Or cities. He loved shows about cities. Buildings. Skyscrapers. He would memorize the heighth of buildings. The dates they were built. Practically an expert.

TERRY: I'm sorry, I don't remember.

FAY: Maybe it will come back to you.

RACHEL: Mom—

FAY: It might come back to her.

RACHEL: *(To* TERRY*)* Don't worry about it.

TERRY: It may. It may come back.

FAY: See?

TERRY: He left a note.

FAY: Oh.

TERRY: *(Handing it to her)* It was left on the night stand. It's addressed to you and your husband.

FAY: It's on motel stationary. Where is this motel?

TERRY: Just outside town. Near the place where you are staying.

FAY: Did we pass it?

TERRY: Yes, you would have passed it.

FAY: Can we go by later? Can I see the room?

TERRY: I suppose...yes, of course, we can go by.

FAY: Is it a nicer place than where we are?

TERRY: Well, no, it's not.

FAY: I wish it was. I wish it was nicer. Hmph...
(Struggling to make out the words in the note.)
I can't read this.

RACHEL: Want me?

TERRY: *(Overlapping with above)* I can read it for you.

FAY: No. Oh...oh...what a sweet, kind note. And in his voice. Listen to this Rachel. It's in his voice. "Dear Mom and Dad, I couldn't think what else to do. Nobody is to blame. Love, Kenny. In case of an emergency call sister, Rachel Browney, 1-312-978-7234. She lives at 514 West Armitage in Chicago. If she's not home, wait until she is." He knew a lot about you, didn't he?

RACHEL: Yes.

FAY: There it is. *(She hands to* RACHEL.*)* So now?

TERRY: We can go down—

FAY: Yes.

TERRY: But it isn't necessary.

FAY: Of course, it is.

TERRY: You can wait—

FAY: What would I wait for?

TERRY: His body is the same as it was found.

RACHEL: I don't think you should go down.

FAY: I think I should. And so I think I will.

TERRY: There are bruises on the face.

FAY: Oh.

TERRY: We think your son had been in some kind of altercation before—

FAY: An altercation?

TERRY: He appears to have been in some kind of a fight—

FAY: A fight? With who?

TERRY: We're not sure. We're doing an investigation.

FAY: An investigation? *(To* RACHEL*)* Did you know this?

RACHEL: No... No, Mom, I didn't.

TERRY: When was your last contact with your son?

FAY: Oh, we talked every week. Every Sunday, I would call. I would call every Sunday. And he was always at home. I can't remember one time when he wasn't at home when I called. *(Suddenly to* RACHEL*)* Why did he put your name on the note?

RACHEL: I don't know.

FAY: He addresses the letter to me and your dad, but then says to contact you.

TERRY: I would think—

RACHEL: *(Overlapping with the above)* He probably—

(Beat)

TERRY: He wanted the news to come from someone you knew.

FAY: Oh. So he was beat up?

TERRY: He was in some kind of altercation.

FAY: And so he checked into a motel and shot himself.

TERRY: Yes.

FAY: Hmph...

TERRY: This was not the first time, Mrs Schorsch. Your son had been beaten a couple of times before.

FAY: Oh.

(She looks at RACHEL. *Beat)*

TERRY: Your son drank a great deal.

FAY: Did he?

TERRY: And that sometimes lead to—

FAY: An altercation.

TERRY: Yes. But we have questioned the man we believe—

FAY: You know who did it?

TERRY: We're fairly certain.

RACHEL: He's been arrested?

TERRY: He's not been charged, no.

RACHEL: Not been charged?

TERRY: We're still investigating.

RACHEL: He denies the charges?

TERRY: Not exactly. It appears to be a case of self-defense.

FAY: Against Kenny? *(She starts to laugh.)* Self-defense against Kenny? *(She continues to laugh.)* I want to meet this man! *(Still laughing, almost hysterically.)* He must be a midget or something. *(Still laughing)* He must be some kind of cartoon character, some kind of stick figure, some kind of ninety pound weakling—

RACHEL: Mom—

FAY: Is he in a wheelchair? Is he some kind of a crippled person? Is he missing a leg? Both his arms? Some kind of blind person? Were his hands tied behind his back?! He has to fight off Kenny in self-defense? Kenny's a little guy, a little skinny guy. Little bitty arms. Little chicken arms. Skinny little legs. And not a mean bone in his body. That is the nuttiest, craziest, dumbest, stupidest thing I've ever heard—more stupid. Most stupid. *(To RACHEL)* You know Kenny— *(To TERRY)* —you've seen Kenny—nobody needed to defend themselves from Kenny. Nobody needed to do that! That's a lie, that's a lie! So you investigate! You investigate that!

RACHEL: She will.

FAY: She'd better.

RACHEL: She will.

TERRY: We will, Mrs Schorsch.

FAY: I'm sure you will. The mother of two. I'm sure you will. How could you live with yourself if you didn't?

TERRY: We're doing all that we can.

FAY: I should hope you would.

TERRY: Frank has been working—

FAY: Who's Frank?

RACHEL: TERRY: *(Simultaneously)*
The other police officer—   He was with me that night.
I told you about him.

RACHEL: Mom?

FAY: What?

RACHEL: Okay?

FAY: *(Suddenly standing)* I need to use the bathroom.

TERRY: *(Standing, too)* It's right there—

FAY: I'm sorry, but I need to freshen up. I can't just—

TERRY: You take all the time—

FAY: I can't go down looking like this.

RACHEL: You look fine—

FAY: I don't look fine—

TERRY: You look nice—

FAY: I can't see Kenny like this. It's been three years. Three years.

TERRY: You do what you need to do.

FAY: This door here?

TERRY: To your left.

FAY: *(As she exits.)* To my left.

TERRY: Right there by the picture of the President.

(FAY exits. Pause. RACHEL sits. Then TERRY sits.)

TERRY: Is she all right?

RACHEL: I think so.

TERRY: It's a tough thing.

RACHEL: Yes, it is.

TERRY: I can't imagine losing one of my mine.

RACHEL: No, I'd rather not imagine it.

TERRY: Yes... Is your mother, okay?

RACHEL: She's all right.

TERRY: This is hard, I'm sure.

RACHEL: Yes. Very. But she's fine. Mom is always fine.

TERRY: Is she?

RACHEL: You have to take my mother with a grain of salt.

TERRY: What?

RACHEL: Nothing. Thanks for your help.

TERRY: It's my job.

RACHEL: And you've done a good one.

TERRY: Thank you. I try. Sometimes too much, I think. But I feel I have to prove myself. All the time.

RACHEL: Don't we all?

TERRY: Oh...well, I suppose. *(Beat)* I like your jacket.

RACHEL: Oh, thank you.

TERRY: Pretty colors.

RACHEL: On sale.

TERRY: Really?

RACHEL: Yes. Fifty percent off.

TERRY: I love sales.

RACHEL: Me, too.

TERRY: And those are such nice colors on you.
I can't wear stuff like that.

RACHEL: Sure, you can.

TERRY: No, I don't think so...I've never been to Chicago.
I've been to Milwaukee and to Indianapolis. I was
in Saint Louis, too, and even that suburb outside of
Chicago—Brookfield. And the zoo. Huge zoo. Walked
for hours and nearly killed my feet. But never been to
Chicago. My husbands says you park your car on the
street and they steal your tires.

RACHEL: *(Laughing)* Really?

TERRY: That's what he says.

RACHEL: I've parked my car on the street many times
and not once have my tires been stolen.

TERRY: Oh. Well, I'll tell him.

RACHEL: You should.

TERRY: Then I will.

(They look at one another. Beat)

TERRY: *(Quietly)* He says there's a lot of black people on
the street.

RACHEL: Oh.

TERRY: That's what he says.

RACHEL: Oh.

TERRY: There's a lot of black people on the street,
he says.

RACHEL: *(Softly)* Oh.

TERRY: But he's still a nice a guy.

(RACHEL *grunts softly.*)

RACHEL: Really...

TERRY: You don't know her well, do you?

RACHEL: Who?

TERRY: Your mother. You don't know her well?

RACHEL: I do.

TERRY: But not very well.

RACHEL: I think I do.

TERRY: But you don't see her much?

RACHEL: Not really. Once in a while. I'm busy. I don't have much...in common. But I know her pretty well.

TERRY: Me, too. The same story.

RACHEL: What's that?

TERRY: When my mom remarried, she turned into another woman and I just stopped seeing her. She suddenly became kind of loud. She suddenly became into herself, for lack of a better way of saying it. Got into the man she married who was a number one bozo-clown. Called himself a poet. I just called him bozo clown. I don't like her new husband and so I just stopped seeing her. An occasional card. A once in a while phone call. My sister's the same way.

RACHEL: Ahhhh.

TERRY: Your brother, too?

RACHEL: I didn't see him much after I left home.... For lots of reasons.

TERRY: He was very troubled.

RACHEL: Yes. I suppose I should have taken more interest...but I didn't. Because, honestly, I didn't really have the interest. I moved away. I got married. I got a job. I had a child.

TERRY: Their name?

RACHEL: Jacob.

TERRY: Jacob. My son is a Jacob!

RACHEL: Really?

TERRY: I love the name. *(Showing a picture on desk)* This is him.

RACHEL: What a pretty child!

TERRY: He's beautiful. And your Jacob?

RACHEL: *(Getting into purse)* I have a few pictures here. *(She takes out a small packet of pictures.)* This is the best one.

TERRY: Oh my God, he's beautiful.

RACHEL: *(Overlapping)* He loves that bunny. *(Handing her another)* He's going off to pre-school.

TERRY: *(Overlapping)* Ahhhhh, I love that little suit he has on. I bet he's smart.

RACHEL: He's already reading, at a third grade level—oh. *(She stops suddenly.)* I'm sorry.

TERRY: Not every kid can be a genius. Now can they?

RACHEL: *(Putting pictures away)* No.

TERRY: Don't be ashamed! He looks like a genius.

RACHEL: Thank you.

TERRY: And it's nice to see that your brother had a family. We just wondered.

RACHEL: We?

TERRY: Me and my sister. We just wondered about him. Where he came from? He stocked the shelves at the Kroeger where my sister works. He told us stories. He told stories about you, particularly. It sounded like you owned Chicago. He was very proud of you.

RACHEL: Ahh. *(Chuckling)* When we were kids, my mother killed a bat that had gotten into the house. She killed it with a broom—beat it to death if you can imagine.

TERRY: I can see it now that you say it. I can see her doing that.

RACHEL: Kenny was so upset, was crying hysterically and screaming for her to stop. Don't kill the bat. He cried easily. Very sensitive little kid. *(Quietly)* I could have been a nicer sister. I could have been. *(In normal voice)* And so my mother beats the thing to death and after she had thrown the bat into the trash, he snuck the body out of the garbage, and he buried it in the backyard. He had a funeral for this dead bat that was killed by my mother. Only then would he stop crying. He asked me to say something at the grave site and so I did. *(Quickly)* "Dear God, Take care of the dead bat and forgive Mom for killing it rather than chasing it to the outside and letting it live." *(Beat)* It was a secret funeral so as not to disturb Mom. Mom would have no patience for funerals. No patience. *(Beat)* And that was my little brother—and my little mother. Little Mama, Mama, Mama—

(FAY enters. TERRY stands.)

TERRY: And there she is.

FAY: I missed a story?

TERRY: About a bat.

FAY: Oh. I think I know this story.

TERRY: And I saw all kinds of pictures of your grandson. He's beautiful. I think he even looks like you.

FAY: Oh... Really? And pictures?

TERRY: Sweet, really sweet.

RACHEL: *(Overlapping with* TERRY*)* I found a couple.

FAY: *(Confused)* Oh...so...so do I look a little better?

RACHEL & TERRY: Yes.

FAY: Yes? Good. So then...I guess...let's go see him.

TERRY: All right.

(They begin to leave.)

TERRY: Oh. *(She stops.)* I remember now. He was watching *Animal Planet*.

FAY: Was he?

TERRY: Yes. It was "Animal Planet.

FAY: He loved "Animal Planet.

TERRY: And that was what he was watching.

FAY: What animal?

RACHEL: Mom, why would she remember that?

TERRY: The orangutan.

FAY: I thought you'd know. *(To* RACHEL*)* See? I thought she would—

TERRY: It just came back to me.

FAY: Yes...well...he loved monkeys. Especially the orangutan. *(She suddenly makes the sound of a monkey.)* He used to make that sound. The sound of the orangutan, he said. He loved their long red hair. Red was his favorite color. And he loved the orangutan's red hair. "They should comb their hair", he'd say! "They look like messy old men." He was one of those people, you know, who are intrigued by simple things. Hmph...good, I'm glad to know. Okay.

TERRY: *(She takes* FAY's *hand,)* I want you to know, Mrs Schorsch, that no matter what you see, I want you to know that no matter how your son may look, I always try to treat each body like a real person, like they're still alive. When I was working with your son, I told him I felt real bad for him. I said "Honey, things just get so hard. You were a cute thing, though. I'm sorry things got you so down." *(Beat)* I just want you to know that I treated him with respect. Some people wouldn't, but that's not me.

FAY: Thank you.

TERRY: This way, please.

(The lights blackout.)

Scene Three

(An hour or so later. FAY *and* RACHEL *come into the motel room.* FAY *goes quickly to the bathroom and closes the door.* RACHEL *stands outside the door. We hear water running. Beat.* RACHEL *listens and then goes to the bed. She lies down. Beat. She gets up and goes to the bathroom door. She listens. Then)*

RACHEL: Are you all right? ...Can I get you anything? ...Mom? ...Mom?

FAY: *(Off/loudly)* NO!

(Beat. RACHEL *goes to the bed. She lies down. The water is still running.* RACHEL *sits back up. Beat)*

RACHEL: *(Softly)* God. Damn it. Damn it. Fucking shit. How did I get into this fucking shit? Fucking shit.
(She gets up and goes to the bathroom door. She listens. Beat)
Mom? *(She goes to her suitcase. She looks for her cellphone.*

She goes through the suitcase. She eventually takes everything out. She mumbles to herself as she searches.) Where is...I don't get it...this doesn't make any sense... *(She looks around the room. She goes through the drawers. She looks under the bed.)* I don't get it.... *(She goes to the bathroom door. Beat.)* Mom? ...Mom? ...Are you okay? ...Can you hear me?

FAY: *(Off)* What?

RACHEL: Are you okay—

(FAY suddenly opens the door. She has a damp cloth that she is using to wash her face.)

FAY: I'm okay. I haven't killed myself if that's what you mean!

(She goes back in. She slams the door. Beat.)

RACHEL: *(Very carefully)* I can't find my cellphone... are you all right in there? Can you hear me? *(Beat)* You don't have it, by any chance.

FAY: *(As she opens the door)* Why would I have it? What would I be doing with it? You need a phone, Rachel, there's one there on the desk. There's a phone. Use that phone. I'm certain it works.

(She goes back in. She slams the door. Beat)

RACHEL: I'm upset, too, Mother. I'm upset, too—

FAY: *(Opening the door.)* What?

RACHEL: Me, too, Mother. I'm upset, too.

(FAY goes to hug RACHEL. She backs up. Beat. Then:)

FAY: *(Softly)* I don't have your phone. And I'm sorry for yelling. *(She goes back in the bathroom. Beat)*

RACHEL: *(Very softly)* Liar.

(She goes to FAY's suitcase. She opens it. She begins to go through it very tentatively at first, and then wildly like she is

*obsessed. At one point, she begins tearing at the clothing.
She stops. Breathless. Almost crying. She regroups and then
begins packing things neatly into place. She says softly to
herself: "Don't come out, yet, Don't come out. Hold on a
little bit." She replaces the suitcase. Then)*

RACHEL: I'm going to check at the front desk. Mom?
I'm going to check at the front desk.

(Beat. RACHEL exits. FAY comes out of the bathroom.)

FAY: *(With washcloth in hand)* Oh. *(She stands there.
She looks at door to adjoining room. She goes to it and listens
again. Beat.)* You can come in, Kenny. If that's you and
I think it is, you can come on in. Mom is dressed. *(She
begins to act as if a very young Kenny has come through the
door and she begins to sing to him and dance with him as
well.)* "Summer's here and the time is right, for dancing
in the street. Dadadadada Chicago, down in New
Orleans, there'll be music, sweet music, there'll be
music everywhere, Kenny, can you hear me? Doesn't
matter what you wear, just as long as you are there, so
come on, Kenny, please, grab a girl, everywhere around
the world, keep dancing, dadadadada, dancing in the
street—dancing in the street. Join a real long line...
dadadada." *(Beat. She waits. She goes over to the bed.
Beat. She puts washcloth over face and screams/cries into it.
She screams/cries again. And then one more time.)* Ohhh,
Kenny, you looked so bad, Kenny. You looked so bad
laying there. I didn't think it was you, you looked so
bad, so different. All bloated and blue. So I'm hoping
you'll come in now so I can see you as you really are.
Come on in, Kenny. Come on in. That motel room,
sweetie, that motel room, I couldn't stand that, Kenny,
that motel room. I don't know what to think that my
son killed himself in such a place. Such an awful place.
Nothing on the wall, really. No pictures, really. I looked
for pictures. I hoped to see what you saw, but... *(She
reaches in her pocket and takes something and holds it up to*

the ceiling. It's a piece of hair.) This isn't your's, is it?
I was hoping it might be. Just little bit of hair. I thought
it might be. It looks gray, though, so I wasn't sure.
Did your hair go a little gray since I saw you. I couldn't
tell, honey, looking at you on that damned gurney
in that awful room, with the terrible lights. They
practically burnt my eyes.

*(Beat. Someone knocks at the other door. FAY freezes.
Someone knocks once again. Beat.)*

FAY: Well—odd. Who is it? Did you forget your card?
I shouldn't let you in as bad as you've been.

(Someone knocks again. FAY talks as if to herself.)

FAY: I'm no letting you back unless you've changed
your attitude. Did you hear me, Rachel? Did you hear
me?

(A knock. As FAY goes to the door.)

FAY: Did you hear me? *(Beat)* Coming.

(FAY goes to the door. She looks through the peephole in door.)

FAY: Oh! *(She opens it.)*

TERRY: *(Off)* I was on my way home—

FAY: Well, come in. Come in. This is a surprise.

(TERRY comes in carrying a few sacks.)

TERRY: I was driving home and I thought—

FAY: You live out this way?

TERRY: Out this way, not too far. But I was on my way—

FAY: Your two children.

TERRY: And my husband.

FAY: Well, you can come in.

TERRY: I thought I would bring you supper.

FAY: Supper?

TERRY: I wanted to bring you and Rachel something to eat. I just thought that after all—what happened—

FAY: That is so nice of you—

TERRY: I may have gotten carried away. *(She chuckles.)* I brought silverware and dishes—

FAY: Dishes?

TERRY: And a table cloth—

FAY: You brought all that—

TERRY: I thought, that, here you are—all by yourself in this town and what you've gone through, the grief and everything that goes with it. So here it is. And here I am.

FAY: Well, lets put it on the table.

(As TERRY *comes all the way in)*

TERRY: I hope this isn't too presumptuous of me.

FAY: Of course not!

TERRY: I went to the store—the grocery store here has a nice selection of products.

FAY: It smells good.

TERRY: Do you want me to set things up?

FAY: You don't have to.

TERRY: I brought everything you might need.

(As she sets up, FAY *just watches her.)*

TERRY: You know, I thought, that with all you have been through, that here you are in a strange town, your son...that, well, I thought it would be a good idea to help you out in some way and when a relative dies, you always bring food. You always try to make things a little more pleasant. I hope you don't mind the way this table cloth looks. It's all they had, but at least the

napkins and plates match, don't they? And this plastic
ware is actually not bad. It doesn't break easily and the
knives actually cut. Not that you'll have to worry too
much about it because I brought a turkey loaf. And
mashed potatoes and green beans. Nothing tough.
I pick this up sometimes for my family and they think
it's great. It smells good, doesn't it?

FAY: Yes.

TERRY: A bottle of wine.

FAY: How nice, but I don't drink.

TERRY: Oh, I'm sorry—

FAY: Never as a matter of fact, but my daughter drinks
so she'll just love that.

TERRY: Good. *(She reaches into a another bag.)* And to
brighten things up a bit—tada!—a small cake with a
few candles.

FAY: How nice of you.

TERRY: A caramel cake.

FAY: I love a caramel cake.

TERRY: I'll set the table.

FAY: Well—

TERRY: I can set the table.

FAY: All right. Can I help you?

TERRY: Sure.

(They begin to get things set-up.)

TERRY: I think you'll find the food to be pretty good.
Very homemade. My sister, she's head cook at
Kroeger's and she has many good recipes. Going there
for your dinner is like going out, really, on a special
occasion. And this turkey meat loaf has a lot of unusual

ingredients that my sister came up with as she
experimented with cooking. The Italian spices.
The rosemary. The chopped onions and pepper.
This wonderful gourmet ketchup that I can't remember
the name of. You can really taste the rosemary in my
sister's recipe. Do you cook?

FAY: I do, but not very well.

TERRY: Now why do I find that hard to believe?

FAY: I really don't. I've worked my entire married life
and so I never really got a feel for it. My husband is a
cook.

TERRY: Really?

FAY: Yes. A very good cook. Simple things. But he likes
to cook. It calms him down.

TERRY: Oh.

FAY: He's the nervous type. Doesn't sleep at night
from worrying. He's that type. Sometimes wakes up
screaming and hollering. I have to get up. I have to
get him a glass of wine. That calms him a little bit.
Sometimes just sitting up and talking to him for a while
will do it, but...people don't help as much you think,
you hope.

TERRY: Ahhh.

(Beat)

| TERRY: | FAY: |
| My husband gets— | He's always been like— |

TERRY: Go ahead.

FAY: He's always been like that. That's all.

TERRY: Yes.

FAY: My son—you knew him?

TERRY: A little.

FAY: You did?

TERRY: Just a little. It's a small town and your son was unusual—different—I don't know—he was nice— I'm sorry. I don't know what I'm saying. I just feel so badly for you.

FAY: Thank you.

TERRY: So badly.

FAY: Thank you.

(She hands TERRY *a kleenex.)*

TERRY: Thanks.

FAY: This was very nice of you, Terry. You're a very nice, very good woman.

TERRY: Well, I try to be...I think of myself as tough, but I'm not as tough as I look. I think of myself as professional, but I'm not as professional as I look.

FAY: You're very professional.

TERRY: Not really.

FAY: Sure you are—

TERRY: My sister keeps telling me I should hook up with her at the Kroeger's, I'd have more fun on the job that way...I sometimes cry about my son.

FAY: Do you, honey?

TERRY: Yes. I worry about what will happen to him. I worry if he'll make it.

FAY: He'll make it.

TERRY: He seems scared. He seems worried all the time—and he's only seven. He has these little worry lines around his mouth, around his forehead. How can an seven year old be worried all the time? Is it his reading problem? Does that worry you when you're seven?

FAY: It might.

TERRY: It seems like I need to do more. Need to figure things out for him.

FAY: He'll make it.

TERRY: He will?

FAY: Look at his mother.

TERRY: Oh.

FAY: Look at her.

TERRY: Thank you.

FAY: Sweet and kind.

TERRY: Thank you.

FAY: Who wouldn't be all right?

TERRY: I feel guilty about him. I feel bad sometimes. I got fat with him—

FAY: You're not fat.

TERRY: Oh, please. I'm fat.

FAY: You're strong looking.

TERRY: I am fat and I know that.

FAY: No.

TERRY: I am fat. And that's that.

FAY: You're really not.

TERRY: Well, you're nice, but I did. I got fat with him and I'm afraid I sometimes resent that and he knows it and so he has a reading problem.

FAY: Oh, well, I'm sure—

TERRY: Well, it's not his fault, is it? It's not his fault.

FAY: Why don't you stay and eat something with us?

TERRY: Oh, no.

FAY: Please stay and eat something with us.

TERRY: I have to go home.

FAY: You don't—

TERRY: I do, really. My kids—

FAY: Just an appetizer? Something—

TERRY: I have laundry to do—

FAY: Your sister's turkey meat loaf—

TERRY: I know, I know—

FAY: Please—

TERRY: No.

FAY: Well—

TERRY: But thank you.

FAY: I don't know who's going to eat all—

TERRY: Well, you could... *(Beat)* Your son would flirt—

FAY: What?

TERRY: He would flirt—

FAY: Flirt?

TERRY: Yes.

FAY: Oh.

TERRY: With the wrong people.

FAY: He would flirt? What?

TERRY: With the wrong people but he was a very nice man.

FAY: Oh.

TERRY: Yes.

FAY: Oh.

TERRY: Yes.

FAY: And these people, these men would beat him up?

TERRY: Yes...I didn't know if you knew about that.

FAY: I didn't know.

TERRY: I thought that you needed to know. I thought if you were to understand—

FAY: Of course.

TERRY: I'm sorry.

FAY: Well, it is upsetting.

TERRY: I'm so sorry.

FAY: So they would beat him up?

TERRY: He would get drunk—

FAY: They would beat him up?

TERRY: Yes.

FAY: For flirting? They beat people up for flirting? I would like to meet these men—

TERRY: Well—

FAY: I would like to meet those men!! I would like to meet them!!

TERRY: I shouldn't have told you.

FAY: Yes, you should have told me. I can take it. I can take anything. But I want to meet all the men who would do such a thing to my son. Where are they? Where do they live?

TERRY: They—

(FAY *suddenly hugs* TERRY *who hugs her back.*)

TERRY: Now sometimes, there is nothing you can do. We both know that, don't we? We both know. There are some things you can't do a goddamn thing about it, no matter what you try to do to change things, to make things better, there's no way to fight it, can't fight it—

FAY: But you know the man—

TERRY: Yes.

FAY: *(Whispering)* You know the man, you can get him, you can get him, you can get him, you can put him in the morgue next to Kenny—

TERRY: I couldn't—

FAY: Please, please, please, please do it. I'm a mother. I'm a mother like you. Like you!

TERRY: OUCH!!! You pinched me!!

(Overlapping with above, FAY *pinches her again.)*

TERRY: Owww! You pinched me again!!

FAY: I don't know what's wrong with me. I didn't mean to!

TERRY: You didn't mean to?

FAY: I'm so sorry. I was frustrated, I wasn't thinking—

TERRY: It hurt. There's going to be a mark.

FAY: I really didn't—

TERRY: I'm trying to help you—

FAY: I didn't. I didn't mean to. Honestly. My son has just killed himself. My son's body is lying in a morgue. My son...

TERRY: All right.

FAY: All right?

TERRY: Calm down. Calm down.

FAY: I'm so sorry.

TERRY: Of course, you are.

FAY: I am not like that.

TERRY: I know you're not. But you need to remember—

FAY: Yes?

TERRY: Don't talk like that. Don't ever act that way. Don't pinch me again. I'm an officer. An officer of the law. And the county coroner and I work for the police and you can get into trouble when you pinch me.

FAY: Could I?

TERRY: Yes.

FAY: You mean go to jail?

TERRY: I do. You can't pinch people, particularly a policewoman, and expect to get away with it.

FAY: I'm sorry. I'm sorry. I've never—

TERRY: Okay—

FAY: I never—

TERRY: Okay, okay. I understand.

FAY: I've never, I swear—

TERRY: Shhhhhh.

FAY: (*Overlapping with* TERRY) Shhhhh.

(*Beat*)

TERRY: Shhhhh. (*Beat*) How 'bout I stay for a bite?

FAY: (*Hugging her*) You'll stay?

TERRY: For a bite.

FAY: Oh, good.

(FAY *kisses her.*)

TERRY: You sit.

FAY: *(As she kisses* TERRY *again)* I'll sit.

TERRY: But let go of me first.

FAY: Oh... *(She giggles and kisses* TERRY.*)* I'm sorry. Ahhh, your little pinch mark.

TERRY: That's okay.

FAY: I lost it for a minute—

TERRY: You don't have to—

FAY: *(Still holding* TERRY'*s arm)* I've been so...and it felt so good to me, Terry. It felt so wonderful. To say it. Get 'em. *(Fiercely)* Get 'em.

TERRY: Yes, I know exactly what you mean.

(They look each other square in the eye.)

TERRY: You want to hang on to me while I dish up?

FAY: *(As she lets go)* Oh—

TERRY: You go right ahead. And I'll dish up.

FAY: This looks so good.

TERRY: And what we don't eat—

FAY: I might eat it all.

TERRY: But we've got to save some for your daughter.

FAY: She won't eat anything.

TERRY: Oh, sure, she will.

FAY: No, she won't.

TERRY: Oh, she smells this—

FAY: She won't. Never. The wine, she'll love the wine.

*(*TERRY *starts to speak.)*

FAY: *(Cutting her off)* How about a story, a funny little story with a happy ending? I love stories with happy endings. And there are so few of them.

TERRY: Well, I—

FAY: What is that saying?

TERRY: What?

FAY: Smile and they all follow along.

TERRY: I don't know it.

FAY: Oh, sure. Smile and they all—

TERRY: *(Suddenly remembering)* —follow you smiling!

FAY: Is that it?

TERRY: That's it.

FAY: I don't think that's it, but it sounds okay—

TERRY: Frown and they all turn against you.

FAY: No, no, cry. I think it's cry.

TERRY: Is it cry?

FAY: You cry and then they all do something else.

TERRY: They cry, don't they?

FAY: *(She got it!)* Cry and they all cry for you!

TERRY: That's it.

FAY: Thought so!!! And so tell me the happy story to make me smile and get others to follow. Do you have a story?

TERRY: *(Befuddled)* Well...I might, I suppose—a funny story—

FAY: A happy ending, right?

TERRY: Oh... yes, very happy.

FAY: So what is it?

TERRY: *(As she prepares for the meal)* Well, yes, once, I had a little shih-tzu dog once—

FAY: Shitzu?

TERRY: Shih-tzu.

FAY: Shitzu?

TERRY: A little Shih-tzu. Little things. Cute little things. Tiny.

FAY: Ahhh.

TERRY: She's out in the yard one day and this great big German Shepherd comes up behind her, puts her head in his mouth and just clamps down, squishing my little shih-tzu's left eye out of its socket—

FAY: No!

TERRY: Yes.

FAY: My stars, my God!

TERRY: It was just dangling there and so I beat off that German Shepherd and rushed her to the vet, but too late. She lost the eye and had her socket stitched up in a permanent fashion, but not once, not once did she complain or cry or growl—

FAY: God bless the shitzus of this world—

TERRY: And so I drove her home and I baked her a turkey meat loaf and she practically ate it in one gulp.

FAY: I'll bet. And mmmm, this is so good.

TERRY: You see, it's comfort food.

FAY: It is.

TERRY: It comforts even the little shih-tzu dog whose eye pops out of her head. *(She takes a bite.)* Oh my God.

FAY: What's that? What's happened?

TERRY: This is not turkey.

FAY: It's not.

TERRY: I told her turkey.

FAY: Well, but this is good.

TERRY: I said turkey, Tammy. Turkey.

FAY: She just got mixed up.

TERRY: But I'm trying to lose weight.

FAY: You look fine.

TERRY: I can't eat this.

FAY: Of course, you can.

TERRY: I can't.

FAY: You can.

TERRY: I can't—

FAY: You eat that. You go ahead. You have a meat loaf for heaven sake—

TERRY: I just can't.

FAY: Look at me, eating this.

TERRY: But I've promised. No fatty red meats! No fatty red meats!

FAY: Break a promise.

TERRY: He grabs my fat.

FAY: He what?

TERRY: He grabs it—here, around my waist— he pinches it—

FAY: Who is this?

TERRY: Jamie.

FAY: That's your husband?

TERRY: Yes.

FAY: That is absurd.

TERRY: He calls me fat.

FAY: I tell you what you do next time he does that. You take some big plate of meat loaf, and you drop it square on his head and then you say, you call me fat one more time and I'll drop the whole frickin kitchen on your head. Now clean up this mess!!! And then you wave your hand like this. Now go ahead. Eat some fatty red meat. *(Beat)* Go On!

TERRY: All right... *(She eats a bit.)* It is good.

FAY: Your sister is a good chef.

TERRY: *(Mocking)* You call me fat one more time and I'll drop the whole fuckin' kitchen on your head.

BOTH: Now clean up this mess!!!

(They both laugh. They eat. They laugh again. Then)

FAY: That's the man, by the way.

TERRY: What?

FAY: That's the man that beat up my son.

TERRY: *(Stopping)* Oh no.

FAY: I'm not saying it was him.

TERRY: It wasn't him.

FAY: It's just the type.

TERRY: Oh, no.

FAY: It's just the type.

TERRY: Oh, I don't think that's so.

FAY: I love this meat loaf.

TERRY: I don't think my husband would ever—

FAY: I'd like the recipe.

TERRY: Well, I—

FAY: I think he would.

TERRY: Oh, I don't think—

FAY: He's the German Shepard—

TERRY: What?

FAY: Men like that. My husband cried when I told him about Kenny. He cried. He used to be the type that would beat someone like Kenny—

TERRY: Oh, I bet—

FAY: But he learned.

TERRY: Oh.

FAY: Now if only my daughter...

(Beat. TERRY *is staring at* FAY. *Then* TERRY *stands.)*

FAY: Are you all right?

TERRY: I just can't stay.

FAY: You can't stay?

TERRY: No, I can't.

FAY: But we just sat—

TERRY: I'm feeling very sick. I think I've been hit by the flu bug. I feel a dizzy spell coming.

FAY: Then lay down, you should lay down.

TERRY: I just need to get out of here.

FAY: What did I—did I—

TERRY: I don't really want to get into it right now—

FAY: I didn't mean to—

TERRY: Well, you did, you did. I bring you food—

FAY: It's lovely—

TERRY: And then you say— *(Quickly)* You are mistaken. You are seriously mistaken!

FAY: I don't know—

TERRY: About my husband.

FAY: I didn't mean to—

TERRY: He wouldn't beat up anybody.

FAY: Well, I wasn't trying to say—

TERRY: Yes, you were and no, he wouldn't.

FAY: I don't think you know for sure.

TERRY: I know for sure.

FAY: I'm sorry if I upset—

TERRY: You did. You did upset me.

FAY: I'm sorry, but I just feel—

TERRY: Well, it is not true.

FAY: All right then. Why can't we—

TERRY: How can you say that, anyway?

FAY: I just think that the man who bullies—

TERRY: My husband doesn't bully—

FAY: It sounds like it to me—

TERRY: He doesn't bully.

FAY: He does. Don't protect him. He doesn't need your protection—

TERRY: He is not a—

FAY: *(Overlapping)* You just said yourself—

TERRY: *(Overlapping)* —Bully. He doesn't. I can't believe I've come all the way over here, just to hear that—

FAY: *(Overlapping with above)* Can we not fight? We just became friends. We're friends, aren't we? Aren't we?

(RACHEL *comes in. They both stop. Then, in the silence,* TERRY *says.)*

TERRY: No, I don't think so. I don't think we are.

FAY: *(Quickly)* Look at what she brought. Isn't this nice? Oh... Did you find your phone?

(Beat)

RACHEL: I have it here.

TERRY: Did you lose your phone?

RACHEL: Someone stole it.

TERRY: Stole it?

RACHEL: Yes. I'd like to report a robbery, if I may.

TERRY: A robbery?

RACHEL: And a suspect.

TERRY: Oh—

FAY: No one stole your phone.

RACHEL: How do you know that, Mother? Why do you know that?

TERRY: You found it—

RACHEL: It was found outside the window.

FAY: You dropped it.

RACHEL: I did not drop it. It was stolen.

TERRY: What makes you think that?

RACHEL: Because it was missing and then later found outside my room—under the window.

FAY: She's in love with a phone. Can you imagine, Terry, being in love with your phone?

TERRY: You had left it in the room?

RACHEL: I just got done saying that—

FAY: Don't talk that way—

RACHEL: I'd be very careful here, Mother—I'd be very careful about what you say right here. Be very careful—I don't know what kind of a stupid, immature game you're playing with me—

FAY: It's a phone—

RACHEL: To stay in touch with my son—

FAY: Your new boyfriend—

RACHEL: Who I just talked to—

FAY: Aha!

RACHEL: Why would I—

FAY: Have you even said hello to the officer? Look at this! Look at this supper she's brought.

TERRY: I can understand why—

FAY: She doesn't need to snap at people. Particularly someone who has brought us a nice supper.

TERRY: Maybe I should leave—

RACHEL: I would like—

FAY: Come over here and enjoy the supper.

RACHEL: I'm not hungry.

TERRY: Maybe later. Meat loaf is really good cold, too.

FAY: You should stay—

TERRY: Oh, no, I still have a long drive—

FAY: You said you were near—

TERRY: This way. Yes. I am. Not far. But my daughter. My son. You two—actually, it's further than I thought.... I, well, goodnight.

FAY: Well, thank you.

TERRY: I'll be here early—

FAY: Yes.

TERRY: We'll go over to your son's apartment.

FAY: Yes.

TERRY: *(To* RACHEL*)* Maybe if you think about it—

RACHEL: What?

TERRY: The phone. It'll come back to you.

RACHEL: Thank you.

TERRY: All right. Tomorrow morning then.

FAY: Good night.

*(*TERRY *exits. Beat.* FAY *goes to the table. She begins to serve herself. She takes her time. She is almost leisurely. She even begins to hum* Dancing in the Street. RACHEL, *meanwhile, lies on the bed turns away from her mother.)*

FAY: *(As she eats.)* You should try some of this. *(She takes a bite.)* Mmmmm, this is so good. This is so good. Come over here and have a bite, Rachel. *(She takes another bite.)* And these beans are so good. They're so soft. They're like mush. MMMMM. I'm going to eat all of it if you don't get over here. There won't be one bite left. *(She takes another bite.)* Mmmmmm, these mash potatoes are the best I've ever had. She must use cream instead of milk. Mmmm, sweet taste, such a sweet taste. This is what the world should be about: making and eating good mash potatoes. Well, I'll just eat here by myself, I don't mind. This is so good, I don't mind that at all. I'd rather have the whole thing to myself. *(She begins to sing.)* "Calling out around the world are you ready for a brand new beat. Summer's here and the time is right, for dancing in the street." I think I'll have some wine. Look at this, Rachel, a nice wine. A lovely sweet wine, it says. It should go well with these potatoes. *(She opens the wine.)* I hate when you have to use a cork screw, don't you? *(She struggles a bit.)* There! Done! Rachel, a little wine? I'll pour you some.... I'll leave it here by the bedstand...it's right here if you want it. *(She pours herself a glass. She tastes it.)* Mmmm, that is so nice and sweet. I

love this! *(She tastes some more.)* Wonderful, Rachel.
This is so wonderful. *(She tastes again.)* I should drink
more often, I guess. "Sally, go 'round the roses, Sally,
go 'round the pretty roses, they won't tell your secret,
they won't tell your secret, they won't tell your secret,
no, the roses won't tell your secret." What a haunting
song. *(Sipping)* Always loved that song. Never knew
what it was about it, but I loved how it haunted me.
Black girls singing. Your brother loved this one.
"I wanna love him so bad, down, down, down, down,
ba-doobee-doo, down, down, down, down, I know
his name, his name is Ken, down, down, down, down,
ba-doobee-doo, down, down, down, down". Your
brother loved that I changed the name. *(Singing)*
"I know his name, his name is Ken. I can't be blamed
for loving him". Black girls singing. Haunted me.
Your brother, too. Should we toast to Kenny, Rachel?
Should we toast to your brother's memory? There's a
glass of wine, right there next to you.

(RACHEL gets up. She starts to pack her bags.)

FAY: What are you doing?

RACHEL: Getting another room.

FAY: Well—

RACHEL: I'll stay with you, Mother, and go to Kenny's
apartment. And I'll help you pack all that needs to
be packed, and help you take care of the necessary
business, the papers, ecetera. I will, however, not stay
in this room with you—

FAY: Well—

RACHEL: I will not do it.

FAY: I'm just—

RACHEL: You steal my phone. And lie about it—

FAY: I did not—

RACHEL: You did.

FAY: I will not—

RACHEL: You lied to the police officer—

FAY: Not one lie—

RACHEL: You said you talked to Kenny every Sunday. That you called him every Sunday, when you hadn't talked to Kenny in over a year.

FAY: How do you know that? How would you know?

RACHEL: Because Kenny was calling me.

FAY: Why—

RACHEL: Why did Kenny ever call? Why did he ever call you?

FAY: He wanted to—

RACHEL: He always wanted money.

FAY: He had things hard—

RACHEL: Yes, that, too. Always had things very hard. But when you said no more money, he stopped calling you and started calling me. Anyway, doesn't matter. I'm getting another room. None of this really matters. For years, I've been saying that. None of this matters and I've worked so hard to keep it that way.

FAY: *(Going to suitcase)* You unpack that stuff right now.

RACHEL: I'm getting another room.

FAY: *(Taking something out of* RACHEL's *suitcase)* You are not leaving this room—

RACHEL: Mom—

FAY: *(Taking another item out of suitcase)* You are not leaving.

RACHEL: Mom—

FAY: I mean that.

RACHEL: Leave that alone.

FAY: *(Overlapping)* You had pictures! You had pictures!!!

RACHEL: Get out of my things!

FAY: Why anyone would wear this—out the window! Out the window!

RACHEL: *(Grabbing* FAY*)* Get the fuck out of my stuff.

(Beat)

FAY: Well. Well. Well. Okay.

RACHEL *(As she packs)* You know Kenny started calling me about once a week—

FAY: Once a week—

RACHEL: *(She packs.)* But never, in all that time, did he ever ask about you—

FAY: I don't believe that.

RACHEL: *(She repacks.)* Not once. In the entire year—

FAY: You're just a big liar. You've turned into a big liar.

RACHEL: *(She packs again.)* I was embarrassed by Kenny, especially as he got older, and kept acting like a child, like a young kid, and he could barely get through school, and he could barely hold down a job, but I didn't berate him like you, I didn't harass him like you, I didn't hate him the way that you did!

(There's a pause. FAY *suddenly flies into* RACHEL *who brings her arms up and over her head to protect herself.* FAY *is incredibly violent, hitting out at* RACHEL *in a random and uncontrolled way; sometimes spanking* RACHEL *as if she is a child.* RACHEL *does NOT hit back, but only tries to cover her face, her head, her body as* FAY *hits her.)*

RACHEL: Mom! Mom! Stop! Stop! Mom! Mom! Mom! Stop it!

FAY: *(Simultaneously to* RACHEL *and hitting as* RACHEL *as she speaks)* You don't say that, goddammit, goddammit, you don't say that, you don't say anything about me, you don't say anything about Kenny, I'll knock you up side of the head, I'll beat you silly, knock you silly, you talk like that, you hear me, Rachel, you hear me, you hear me?!

*(*RACHEL *has been knocked to the floor.* FAY *runs to the door and opens it.)*

FAY: *(Shouting)* I would like a room change, please!! A room change!!

(The cellphone rings. Both women freeze. The phone continues to ring. FAY *comes back into the room. She closes the door. The phone rings.* RACHEL *remains on floor. The phone rings again.* FAY *moves to it.* RACHEL *is still.)*

FAY: *(Exhausted)* Do you want me to...?

(She finds the phone. It rings.)

FAY: Do you want me to...?

(It rings. She answers it.)

FAY: Hello, Rachel Browney's phone. *(She listens.)* Jacob? It's grandma, Jacob. Grandma Schorsch... Yes. Do you know me? Do you know me? How are you, honey? How are you? Grandma's fine. She's fine. I never see you. I never see you. I never see you!!! And I am so glad to talk to you.... She's right here, honey. She's laying down, but I'm sure she'll be glad to talk to you. I am sure glad to hear from you. Here's your mommy. *(To* RACHEL*)* Rach...you want to talk to Jacob? He's on the phone. Here he is. Let me help you up. *(To Jacob)* Your Mom is so tired, but she's getting up right now. So what did you do today?

(Beat as she listens and helps RACHEL *get up.)*

FAY: Did you? Did you? *(She laughs.)* I'll bet.
(She chuckles.) Did you really? I bet that was fun.
Ohhh, that's a great game, isn't it? I love that game.
You tell your mother to bring you to see me and I
will play that game with you. Yes. That would be fun.
I never see you. I never see you. I never see you. Okay.
Soon. Here's your mother, honey. Grandma loves you.
She loves you, she loves you, she loves you, she loves
you, she loves you.

(She hands the phone to RACHEL.*)*

RACHEL: *(Who sits on edge of bed)* Jacob? Yes. *(Beat)* Yes.
(Beat) Yes.

(As she talks, FAY *runs out of the room and returns with ice
which she will wrap into a washcloth.)*

RACHEL: *(To Jacob with brief beats between each sentence)*
Yes. Uh-huh. Yes. Yes. Yes. I will. Mommy will. Fine.
You make sure you do. Listen to everything he says.
Yes. Yes. Yes, she is. I will. I will, honey. I will, Jacob.
I will, I promise. I will kiss Grandma. And hug her, too.
I am. I am, Jacob. I'm kissing Grandma right now.

FAY: She's kissing me, Jacob. Kiss, kiss back. She's
hugging me, too. Ohhh, what a nice hug!!!

RACHEL: *(To Jacob)* I'm going to go now, but I will talk
to you right before I go to bed, okay? Right before.
Listen to your dad now. Me, too, honey. I love you, too.

FAY: I love you, Jacob!

RACHEL: *(To Jacob)* Tonight. Yes. Bye-bye, sweetie.
(She hangs up.)

FAY: Ahhh, honey.

(She sits on the bed next to RACHEL. *She lifts ice pack up to*
RACHEL *who flinches at first.)*

FAY: I'm done, honey. I'm done. Mom loves Rachel. She loves you. Come on.

(As she coaxes RACHEL *to lay her head in her lap.)*

FAY: Come on now. Come on. You don't want to go home with a big black eye, do you? I'm done, sweetie. I'm done. Come on.

*(*RACHEL *lays her head in* FAY's *lap.)*

FAY: It was so good to talk to him. He sounds so grown-up, I could not believe it. But a thrill for me. What a big thrill. I can't see him sometime soon? Sometime?

RACHEL: No.

FAY: Oh.

RACHEL: No. Never.

FAY: Oh. Oh. I thought not. I thought I probably couldn't. I thought that. *(Beat)* You shouldn't say those kinds of things about your brother, Rachel. You know that by now, don't you? Don't you? Don't you?

RACHEL: Yes.

FAY: Thank God, you're tough. Thank God for that. I've got one tough kid. One kid who is going to make it through. *(Beat)* Boy, you know, your dad couldn't take it, Rachel. He couldn't take it. That's where your brother got it from. Not like you and me. We can take it. *(She lifts the ice pack.)* It doesn't look too bad. I think by tomorrow, if I keep this pack here like this, it'll hardly be noticeable. You can keep your head right here in my lap if that's okay. I sure don't mind. I've missed being a mother if you want to know. I've really missed it. And you know what? I bet you've missed being a big sister, too, haven't you? I'll bet you have. Kenny was just a sweet thing, Rachel, that's all. He was just a sweet thing. He never knew any better. You know that. He never did. Wasn't he always sweet when he asked for money?

RACHEL: Yes.

FAY: Wasn't he?

RACHEL: Yes.

FAY: He was, and such helpless sorrow to kill himself like that. He knew more than we thought. Didn't he?

RACHEL: Yes.

FAY: Don't you think?

RACHEL: Yes.

FAY: So tell me a story. Do you have a story?

RACHEL: Yes.

FAY: Do you?

RACHEL: Yes, I do.

FAY: Finally. So tell me.

RACHEL: I slapped Kenny once.

FAY: No!

RACHEL: I slapped him. Hard. When he jerked out of my hands. And tried to run away. I slapped him so hard it made his face red.

FAY: Well.

RACHEL: And then he fell to the ground. Trying to get away from me. That's all he knew to do. Get away. Get away. Like a very small and blind animal.

FAY: Oh.

RACHEL: And when I finally pulled him back into me, I said: The Next Time You Do That I'm Going To Kill You!

FAY: Well...sometimes you need to say that to get people to do what they're supposed to do. Even to Kenny.

(The door to the adjoining room opens.)

FAY: And so there he is. Come on in, Kenny. We're glad to see you. Your sister and I. Come on in. Nice to have both of my kids here at the same time. That's been years and years ago. So come on in, honey. Your sister and I are waiting to see you.

*(*FAY *begins to hum and sing* Dancing in the Streets. *Lights fade.)*

END OF PLAY